OXFORD

Revising AQA GCSE

English Literature

Peter Buckroyd

Specification **A**

AQA GCSE English Literature

Foundation and Higher Tiers

OXFORD
UNIVERSITY PRESS

Great Clarendon Street, Oxford OX2 6DP

Oxford University Press is a department of the University of Oxford.
It furthers the University's objective of excellence in research, scholarship,
and education by publishing worldwide in

Oxford New York

Auckland Bangkok Buenos Aires Cape Town Chennai
Dar es Salaam Delhi Hong Kong Istanbul Karachi Kolkata
Kuala Lumpur Madrid Melbourne Mexico City Mumbai Nairobi
São Paulo Shanghai Taipei Tokyo Toronto

Oxford is a registered trade mark of Oxford University Press
in the UK and in certain other countries

British Library Cataloguing in Publication Data

Data available

ISBN 0 19 831895 2

3 5 7 9 10 8 6 4 2

Typeset and assembled by Blenheim Colour Ltd, Eynsham, Oxford

Printed in Italy by Rotolito Lombarda

For Curly

CONTENTS

Preparing for your examination

There are two sections in your English Literature examination. Section A is based on the post-1914 prose text you have read, and Section B on the pre-1914 and post-1914 poetry.

The most important thing is for you to get to know the texts as well as you can. All the notes you have made during the course, all the thinking you have done, all the discussions you have had with your teachers and with other people will have helped to form a lot of ideas in your head and should have made sure that you have good knowledge of the texts.

But you need to be sure that you know them *for yourself*. And the only way to do this well is to spend time reading and re-reading your texts. By the time you get into the exam room you want to be able to remember as much as you can about the details of the texts, and so it's a good idea to get to know bits of the texts very well indeed. It doesn't take you very long to read four or five poems – only a few minutes – and if you do this each day from the time you start revising to the day before the exam then you will get to know those poems extremely well and be able to refer to the very best bit of evidence you can find in them to support the points you want to make.

The same is true of the prose texts. Get to know several short passages of the text very well. Re-read those passages plenty of times so that you know them like the back of your hand. Of course, it also helps to read the whole text again as many times as you can, but you can do effective revision by making sure that you know key episodes very well. And make sure that you think about how the writers achieve their effects. Don't just concentrate on the events, or the characters and their relationships.

Tip! *Knowing the texts back to front is the best recipe for success in the exam.*

You also need to be clear about what you're going to be tested on, and it's useful to look carefully at the Assessment Objectives in your revision to make sure that you are clear what you will be asked about.

To begin with, then, I'm going to take you through the Assessment Objectives. Then there will be some pages on each of the texts that are set for the exam. You will only be studying **one** of the prose texts (either the short stories or one of the novels) and you will be doing **either** the poems of Clarke and Heaney **or** the poems of Duffy and Armitage, so you will only need to use those sections that apply to the texts you are studying. Everyone will be doing the pre-1914 poetry bank.

After I have given you some pointers about what to think about in each of your texts, I will then look at some aspects of examination technique which should help guide you in your revision.

Peter Buckroyd

Assessment Objectives and how to meet them

One of the Assessment Objectives has been tested in your pieces of coursework and is not tested again specifically in the examination:

Assessment Objective 4: Relate texts to their social, cultural, and historical contexts and literary traditions.

However, this shouldn't stop you from writing about contexts or literary traditions if it is relevant to the task you are set, because such comments can always count for 'respond to texts critically'.

The Assessment Objectives for the examination are:

❏ **1:** Respond to texts critically, sensitively, and in detail, selecting appropriate ways to convey your response, using textual evidence as appropriate.
❏ **2:** Explore how language, structure, and forms contribute to the meanings of texts, considering different approaches to texts and alternative interpretations.
❏ **3:** Explore relationships and comparisons between texts, selecting and evaluating relevant material.

Note *All these terms will be explained in the following pages.*

Assessment Objectives 1 and 2 are tested in both sections of the paper. Assessment Objective 3 is tested only if you are writing about the *Anthology* short stories for the prose, but it is tested on all the poetry.

Notes

It is worth breaking these Objectives down to see the kinds of things you might write about. Look at the parts of the Assessment Objectives in the panels below, and read the bullet points to see what you need to do.

Assessment Objective 1

Respond to texts critically, sensitively, and in detail.

- Know the details of the texts very well to be able to support the points you want to make.
- Have an overview of the text.
- Think about the writer's purposes.
- Try to put yourself on the writer's wavelength.
- Think for yourself.
- Draw some inferences and conclusions.
- Think about *how* the writer writes, as well as *what* he or she writes.
- Be able to comment on such aspects of the text as:
  - the characters
  - their relationships
  - how these develop
  - how the writer uses them to bring out ideas
  - the settings
  - relationships between characters and their environments
  - the thoughts, ideas, and feelings of the characters
  - the thoughts, ideas, and feelings of the writer.

Select appropriate ways to convey your response.

- Be sure to answer the question.
- Plan what you are going to say carefully.
- Make sure you develop an argument in your essay.
- Use literary terminology accurately.
- Make sure that everything you write is relevant to the set task.
- Cover as wide a range of relevant material as you can.

Use textual evidence as appropriate.

- Quote accurately and relevantly to support your points.
- Use a wide range of brief quotations or references to the text, rather than a few long ones.
- Analyse what can be seen about the writer's methods and effects in the quotations you use.
- Make sure that your textual references come from a wide range of places in the text.

Assessment Objective 2

Explore how language, structure, and forms contribute to the meanings of texts.

- Think about openings, endings, the sequence of the plot.
- Think about climaxes and turning points.
- Consider such features as **simile**, **metaphor**, **images**, **extended images**, **symbolism**, **word clusters** (semantic fields), **alliteration**, **assonance**, use of the **pathetic fallacy**, kinds of description. In poetry, write about such devices as **rhyme**, **rhythm**, use of **blank verse**, the **sonnet** form, **narrative**. (See the Glossary on page 63 for an explanation of these and other literary terms.)
- Make sure you always comment in detail on the *effect* or *possible effects* of the writer's choices of these techniques.
- Link the device you have identified to the effect, and to the meanings that are created by its use.

Consider different approaches to texts and alternative interpretations.

- Think about different readers' responses to the text.
- Look out for double meanings, puns, ambiguities.
- Think about what the effect of the text might be on different readers (e.g. depending on their gender, ethnicity, social background, religion).
- Consider how your response to the text is influenced by your own experiences.
- Be aware that the writer (especially in poetry) may be asking you to think of more than one thing at the same time.

Assessment Objective 3

Explore relationships and comparisons between texts (this is only for the short stories and the poetry).

- Look for similarities and differences between texts.
- Compare and contrast content, ideas, themes, the writer's purposes, characters, settings, the writer's techniques, beginnings, endings, feelings, your own response, structure, forms.

Select and evaluate relevant material.

- Plan your work carefully.
- Identify the key words of the task.
- Select as many different relevant points to make and areas to consider as you can.
- Make sure that everything you write is relevant to the task.
- Make sure you explore the *purposes* of the writer's choices.
- Make sure you examine the *effect* or *effects* of those choices.

You will see that these Assessment Objectives are not separate. They overlap. Use them to check that you are looking for all the relevant material, but don't separate them out while you are writing. Concentrate instead on identifying the key words of the task and on using these for your plan.

Short stories in the *Anthology*

You must answer **one** out of a choice of **three** questions on the short stories in the *Anthology*. This means that you need to know all seven of the stories really well if you are going to have the maximum choice in the examination. Because at least one short story is named in each question, you need to know at least five very well if you are going to be sure of having a choice of questions. All the questions are likely to ask you to **compare**, so it is useful in revision to think about the stories in pairs. Of course these pairs are not in any way fixed. Which story goes with which depends very much on the question you are considering. Any story could be paired with any other one.

Checklist ✓

You might be asked about anything in the examination, but here are some areas which connect some stories and which you should think about while you are revising:

- ✔ relationships between parents and children
- ✔ what children experience
- ✔ relationships between grandparents and children ('Flight', 'Chemistry')
- ✔ conflict between generations
- ✔ the experience of growing up
- ✔ the behaviour of members of the same family
- ✔ family tensions
- ✔ strong feelings which characters experience
- ✔ misunderstandings
- ✔ disappointments
- ✔ the ways the writers use settings
- ✔ symbolism (for example, the pigeons in 'Flight', war in 'Superman and Paula Brown's New Snowsuit', the shoes in 'Your Shoes', the dog Snort in 'Growing Up', fishing in 'The End of Something', the boat in 'Chemistry', the snowdrops in 'Snowdrops')
- ✔ the ways the opening of each story sets up expectations, and the extent to which these expectations are fulfilled in the story as a whole
- ✔ the effects of the endings
- ✔ the ways many of the stories hinge on a turning point, or more than one turning point
- ✔ first-person narratives ('Superman and Paula Brown's New Snowsuit', 'Your Shoes', 'Chemistry'; the way 'Snowdrops' is told from the child's point of view though in the third person)
- ✔ third-person narratives (the other stories)
- ✔ how the writers build suspense
- ✔ the appropriateness of the titles.

Here are some questions to think about when you are revising each of your short stories in order to be able to compare them.

'Flight'

- ❏ How does the grandfather feel about the pigeons and how do you know?
- ❏ How does the relationship between the grandfather and the pigeons reflect his relationship with his granddaughter?
- ❏ Why do you think the writer describes the season as 'this warm end-of-summer month'?
- ❏ How is the dovecote a 'refuge' for the grandfather?
- ❏ How does the writer show the tensions between the grandfather and his daughter by the language that is used?
- ❏ What do you think is implied by what the grandfather says in lines 68–69? How do these lines show some of his feelings and attitudes? How are these feelings and attitudes also shown elsewhere in the story?
- ❏ How do the grandfather and his daughter think differently about marriage? How is this shown?
- ❏ Why do you think the writer uses the phrase 'their lying happy eyes' in line 112?
- ❏ How does the writer reveal the grandfather's mixed feelings in lines 118–123?
- ❏ In what ways are lines 133–134 important in the story as a whole?
- ❏ Why do you think the writer sets the early part of the story in 'sunlight' (line 2) but ends it with 'the shelter of night' (line 143)?
- ❏ What feelings are expressed in the last three lines of the story?
- ❏ Why do you think the writer chose to end the story like this?

'Superman and Paula Brown's New Snowsuit'

- ❏ The story begins with mention of the war. Why do you think the writer includes several references to the war?
- ❏ Why are the girl's technicolour dreams important and how do her dreams change during the course of the story?
- ❏ In what ways does Uncle Frank seem like Superman to the girl? How does this change through the story?
- ❏ Why does the writer choose to describe the school playgrounds as 'barren gravel playgrounds' (line 31)?
- ❏ How does the writer build up a picture of Sheldon in lines 37–46?
- ❏ In lines 48–49, why do you think the narrator says 'David couldn't see his [Uncle Frank's] likeness [to Superman] as clearly as I did'? What does this show about the narrator?
- ❏ In the first 64 lines of the story how does the writer show the age of the narrator (about 12) by the ways she has the narrator speak and the things that the narrator says?
- ❏ What do lines 65–68 show about the differences between adults' and children's responses to the war?
- ❏ What do you think are the different reasons for the writer setting the story in winter?
- ❏ How does the writer show the narrator's loss of innocence between lines 84 and 96 and then in the rest of the story?
- ❏ How do the girl's dreams change and why?

❏ Explain how the following sentence (lines 121–122) can be read both literally and metaphorically: 'The dull, green light of late afternoon came closing down on us, cold and final as a window blind.'

❏ In lines 138–140 the outside and the house are contrasted. Why does the writer do this? Are the girl's expectations about 'home' fulfilled in the rest of the story?

❏ In lines 69–70 the snow was melting. In line 167 the windows are frosty again. How does the writer's use of the weather here reflect the narrator's feelings and state of mind?

❏ What do you think are the narrator's responses to what Uncle Frank says in lines 176–178? How do you know?

❏ Look carefully at all the images, similes, and metaphors in the last paragraph. What effects do they create?

❏ Why do you think the writer ends the story as she does?

❏ What are the different meanings you can make out of the last sentence?

❏ Why do you think the writer chose this title for her story?

❏ What ideas and feelings are brought out about the relationships between parents, other relatives, and children in the story as a whole?

'Your Shoes'

❏ This story begins by establishing the first-person speaker. Why do you think the narrator says 'I' three times in the first sentence?

❏ The form of this story is a dramatic monologue – monologue because one person tells the story and there are no other voices. How does the writer make the story 'dramatic'? What do you think the 'drama' is about?

❏ Look at the first 13 lines of the story. What different aspects of the narrator's character are brought out in these lines, and what methods has the writer used to bring them out?

❏ How does the writer show the mother's intense feelings in lines 19–23?

❏ In lines 33–41 the writer breaks some of the usual conventions of written English. Find some of them and say what effects they create. Why, for example, do you think there are so many commas where in conventionally written English there would be full stops? How might this device reflect the ways the mother thinks and feels?

❏ In lines 64–65 the mother says 'We've given you everything a child could possibly want'. In what ways do you find this sentence ironic, given the details in the rest of the story?

❏ In lines 85–86 the mother says 'When your father called you a dirty slut he didn't mean you to take it personally'. What do you think the mother means by this? What does it show about her? What does it also show about the father?

❏ When the narrator writes about her own mother she doesn't seem to realize that some parallels can be seen between her relationship with her own mother and her daughter's relationship with her. What similarities can you find between what the narrator says about her mother and her own behaviour?

❏ In the paragraph that begins on line 134, what does the mother reveal about her relationship with her husband?

❏ Are some parallels implied in the story between the father's relationship with his daughter and the mother's relationship with her own father?

❏ What do you think the parallels are, and what evidence can you find to support your ideas?

❏ Lines 167–170 seem to imply what it was that gave rise to the confrontation which led to the girl running away. What is suggested by these lines?

❏ The mother seems to have thrown her own mother's shoes away on the same day that she bought new shoes for her daughter. What does this suggest?

❏ How are shoes important throughout the story, both literally and as a metaphor?

❏ Why do you think the writer ends her story with the sentence in line 191?

❏ Think about the title again. 'Your Shoes' seems to imply that they are the girl's shoes. How could you also see them, just as importantly, to be the mother's shoes?

❏ The story is filled with sentences that imply things without stating them. Find some of these and comment on the effects created by the writer's inclusion of them. Here are a few to start with:

   ◆ 'I'm not cruel.' (line 12)
   ◆ 'In their proper places, no fuss, like a husband and wife.' (lines 29–30)
   ◆ ' . . . who'd have you and what could you possibly do?' (lines 42–43)
   ◆ 'Some pile of filth.' (line 83)
   ◆ 'They are perfect because they are new, they've never been worn.' (lines 132–133)
   ◆ 'At night you cried so much, in the end I used to shut the door on you and go back downstairs.' (lines 147–148).

'Growing Up'

❏ In what ways is this a good title for the story? Which characters arc growing up and in what ways?

❏ When Robert Quick thought the girls had gone to meet him and he had missed them, 'this gave him pleasure and dismay'. Why do you think this was?

❏ In what ways does he experience both 'pleasure' and 'dismay' in the story as a whole?

❏ In lines 53–54 it says 'At fifty-two, having lost most of his illusions, he was good at making the best of things'. How does he 'make the best of things' in the story as a whole?

❏ How does the writer present the gradually increasing sense of violence in the story from lines 63 onwards?

❏ Lines 117–119 seem to mark a turning point in the story. How does the mood change after those lines?

❏ How do you account for the giggles of the girls in lines 112 and 121?

❏ How does the writer show the change from violence to 'games' after line 128?

❏ Why do you think Robert Quick wants to escape to male company?

❏ Why do you think the writer chose to end the story as he does, in lines 177–179?

❏ How satisfying an ending do you find the last line of the story and why?

❏ In what ways can the story be seen as about Robert Quick's self-discovery?

❏ What other key themes can you find in the story?

'The End of Something'

- What is established about Hortons Bay in the opening paragraph of the story?
- Why do you think the writer begins his story with the description of Hortons Bay?
- What do you notice about the conversations between Nick and Marjorie? Look closely at the language they use and what they say to each other.
- In what ways is line 30, 'She loved to fish. She loved to fish with Nick', significant in the story as a whole? Why do you think the second statement was included after the first?
- What is shown about the relationship between Nick and Marjorie and how?
- Why is line 102 '"Isn't love any fun?"' a surprise when it is said?
- In many ways lines 36–37 seem to be unimportant when they are said. In what ways can they be seen to carry more significance when you have finished reading the story as a whole?
- What other statements or lines in the story seem to mean more when you read the story a second time, and why?
- Why do you think the writer chose to end the story with the surprise entry of the mysterious Bill?
- Look at some examples of how simple sentences begin to mean much more than you thought they did at first.
- Why do you think Nick fails to answer Bill's question at the end of the story?
- Why do you think the writer chose fishing on a lake as the setting for much of his story?
- Can the lake, fishing, and the shore be seen as metaphorical or symbolic in any way?
- Why do you think the writer chose to have his story take place at night time?
- In what ways is the title an appropriate one for the story?

'Chemistry'

- Lines 13–16 talk about the relationship between boy, mother and grandfather. How is this patterning reflected in the story as a whole?
- The loss of the boat is the boy's 'first loss' (line 26). What other losses does he experience during the course of the story?
- What do you think is meant by line 29, which says the mother was 'white, as if she had seen something appalling'?
- How are the central family tensions in the story shown by the paragraph in lines 32–36? How are these tensions developed in the story?
- In what ways is the garden shed important to the grandfather?
- What did you understand by lines 67–68 ('But if I really believed Father was gone for ever – I was wrong') when you first read them, and what do you understand by them now?
- Why do you think the grandfather might take a 'secret, vengeful delight in my father's death' (line 72)?
- Why do you think the writer reminds you in lines 77–78 of the picture he created in lines 13–16?
- What are the most significant events which happen to the boy during the course of the story, the ones that seem to change him?

❏ How does the writer present the family tensions in lines 90–101?

❏ How is the special relationship between the boy and his grandfather shown in lines 136–142?

❏ Why do you think the grandfather thought that the boy would visit him in his garden shed?

❏ The grandfather explains a lot about change. Why is this idea of change so important in the story?

❏ How does the writer create dramatic tension in line 201? How do you think differently about this line when you have read the whole story?

❏ What other examples of suspense building can you find in the story?

❏ Why do you think the boy wanted to hurt Ralph?

❏ In line 254 the mother says "'I'll explain'". What might she have explained, and why do you think the writer writes in such a way that she doesn't?

❏ What do you think the boy means in lines 257–9 when he says 'But all the other things that should have been explained – or confessed – she never did explain'. What might these things have been, from the boy's point of view?

❏ Whom does 'him' refer to in line 284? Is this in any way ambiguous? Why do you think the writer chooses not to name the person?

❏ Look carefully at the language of the last paragraph of the story. Why do you think these images and details were chosen for the ending, and why do you think the story ends with this last sentence?

❏ What does the writer leave you thinking and feeling?

❏ Why does the writer choose not to present the events chronologically as they happened? What is the effect of the time shifts?

❏ In what ways do you think that 'Chemistry' is an appropriate title for the story?

'Snowdrops'

❏ The snowdrops keep being mentioned throughout the story. Why are they so important to the boy?

❏ The story is told from the boy's point of view. The reader is told what he does, thinks and feels. Why do you think the writer chose to tell the story in the third person rather than the first person?

❏ What different things does the reader understand that the boy doesn't? How does the writer create this sense of dramatic irony?

❏ Examine some details which present things from a child's point of view and consider the effect this has.

❏ The bacon in the sandwich seems different but is the same. How does the writer explore this idea in the story as a whole?

❏ Why do you think the writer spends so long on the paragraph about the boy's drawing of the robin (lines 103–117)?

❏ Why do you think the boy 'felt a slow, sad disappointment' (line 188)?

❏ Line 194 says 'The boy began to see their fragility'. How does this take on more meaning for the reader than it has for the boy when you think about the story as a whole?

❏ Why do you think the writer ends the story with the children being 'frightened'?

❏ Children often sense that something is wrong without understanding what. How is this shown in the story?

❏ In what ways do you think the snowdrops are symbolic in the story?

Writing about the short stories

Because you will have to compare the short stories in the examination,
I have suggested that it's useful for you to be thinking about them in pairs
while you are revising and then switch the pairs around so that you can begin
to see a range of ways in which the stories are similar and different, both in
terms of what they are about and in terms of the ways they are written.

Tip!

*When it comes to the exam you will have 45 minutes to write about your
two stories. It's important that you spend five minutes making a plan so
that you can find some precise similarities and differences between them,
depending on what question you are asked.*

The exam question is bound to test your understanding of what the stories
are about, but it will also test you about how each writer presents this
material.

You can use the list I gave you at the beginning of this section, which looked
at some similarities between the stories, as a starting point for your revision.
I have taken you through most of these things in my questions on each story
individually.

It would be useful for you to practise making some plans so that you have a
method which will help you to answer the question effectively. Use two
columns to help you to find some similarities and differences. Then when
you write your essay you can order your points in the best way possible so as
to link them into a developing argument. Once you have decided on the best
order you can go through each of the areas in turn, drawing evidence from
both stories.

Notes

Let's take an example.

Question

How do the writers of 'Paula Brown's New Snowsuit' and one other story present the relationships between adults and children?

Points of interest	'Paula Brown's New Snowsuit'	Story: _____
What the relationships are		
1st or 3rd person		
Key events		
Turning points		
How the relationships change/develop		
Methods of showing feelings		
How description shows relationships		
Metaphor/simile/symbolism to show relationships		
Ideas the writers have		
Purposes of the stories		
How things have changed by the end		

Use the following table to compare two other stories. Add some more points of interest to compare and contrast.

Points of interest	Story: _____	Story: _____
What the relationships are		
1st or 3rd person		
Key events		
Turning points		
How the relationships change/develop		
Methods of showing feelings		
How description shows relationships		
Metaphor/simile/symbolism to show relationships		
Ideas the writers have		
Purposes of the stories		
How things have changed by the end		

Novels

For the revision of your chosen novel you should read the whole text as many times as you can. You should also make sure that you know several key passages well so that you can refer to them if they are relevant to your answer.

Checklist ✅

In each of the key passages you choose, you should think about:

✔ how the characters are presented
✔ how the characters behave
✔ any relationships that are shown between them
✔ where the passage is set
✔ how the setting is significant to what happens in the story
✔ how the writer's choice of language brings out feelings
✔ how the writer brings out themes or ideas important to the text as a whole
✔ how the passage marks a significant stage in the novel
✔ how the passage marks a significant point in the development of the characters involved in it
✔ the effect of any similes, metaphors, symbols
✔ other passages that this one makes you think about
✔ where the passage fits, in terms of the shape and the structure of the whole novel.

In addition is it useful to think about the text as a whole in terms of some of these:

◆ what important characters say and do
◆ how key relationships change and develop
◆ the use of minor characters
◆ how the writer uses different settings to bring out ideas and feelings
◆ the importance of key events in the novel
◆ why the writer orders the events in the way that he or she does
◆ how the writer shows ideas, thoughts, and feelings by means of the language characters speak
◆ how the writer shows ideas, thoughts, and feelings by the use of description
◆ key images, metaphors, symbols in the novel
◆ why the novel starts in the way it does
◆ why the novel finishes in the way it does
◆ what you are left thinking and feeling at the end of the novel
◆ any different interpretations of the novel you can think of and what evidence you might use to support these
◆ what you think the writer's various purposes are in writing the novel
◆ the appropriateness and significance of the novel's title
◆ your own responses to the characters, relationships, ideas, and themes in the novel and why you have these responses.

In the pages that follow I shall outline some of the things that you might like to think about while you are revising your novel.

To Kill a Mockingbird

Characters, characters' roles, and relationships:

- Atticus and his role as a single parent and as a lawyer
- Jem (and his relationships with Atticus, Scout, Dill, Mrs Dubose)
- Scout (and her relationships with Atticus, Jem, Dill, Miss Maudie)
- Tom Robinson
- Bob Ewell (and his relationships with Atticus, Mayella, Tom Robinson)
- Boo Radley (and his relationship with the children, his father)
- Calpurnia
- what minor characters reveal: e.g. Mrs Dubose, Miss Maudie, Heck Tate, Dolphus Raymond, the Cunninghams
- different groups of people in society: blacks, whites, white trash, the Missionary Circle ladies, neighbours.

Key events:

Ask yourself what each of the following key events shows you about:
- the characters, their relationships, and attitudes
- Jem and Scout's increasing understanding and maturity
- themes and ideas important to the novel as a whole
- the writer's methods of influencing what you think and feel
- the writer's uses of language which make you think and feel what you do
- the nature of Maycomb society
- why you think the event comes at the stage of the novel that it does
- what you think the writer's purposes are in including this event.

Here are some key events which are useful for you to look at in detail, and where you should consider the points above:
- the knot-hole
- Scout at school with Miss Caroline
- Jem's pants
- Miss Maudie's fire
- Atticus and Tim Johnson
- Jem and Mrs Dubose
- the visit to First Purchase Church
- the gang outside Maycomb jail
- the encounter with Dolphus Raymond
- Tom Robinson's trial
- the missionary circle tea party
- the death of Tom Robinson
- the death of Bob Ewell
- Boo Radley and the ending.

Themes and ideas:

Think about as wide a range of material as you can, where you could write interestingly about each of the following:
- legal and moral justice
- growing up

- prejudice and discrimination
- the nature of society
- the role of the outsider
- parenthood
- leadership
- respect
- literal and metaphorical barriers
- racism.

Language:

- different people's speech
- the uses of description
- the symbol of the mockingbird
- ironies you can find
- how the changes and maturing of the children are shown.

Structure:

- the effect of the order of events
- the pace of the story
- climaxes you can find
- turning points you can find
- the ways one situation reminds you of another
- ideas, thoughts, and feelings established in the opening chapter
- ideas, thoughts, and feelings established in the last chapter.

Of Mice and Men

Characters, characters' roles, and relationships:

- George (and his relationships with Lennie and with the other migrant workers)
- Lennie (and his relationships with George, other people, pets)
- Curley (and his relationship with his wife)
- Crooks (and his relationships with others)
- Candy (and his relationship with his dog)
- what minor characters reveal: e.g. Slim, Carlson, Whit.

Key events:

Ask yourself what each of these key events shows you about:
- the characters, their relationships, and attitudes
- Lennie and George's position
- themes and ideas important to the novel as a whole
- the writer's methods of influencing what you think and feel
- the writer's uses of language which make you think and feel what you do
- the position, lifestyle, hopes, and disappointments of migrant workers
- why you think the event comes at the stage of the novel it does
- what you think the writer's purposes are in including this event.

Here are some key events which are useful for you to look at in detail, and where you should consider the points above:
- the opening descriptive section of the novel
- the first section where the reader meets Lennie and George

- ◆ Lennie's dream for the future
- ◆ the conversation of the ranch hands in the bunkhouse
- ◆ Lennie and the puppy
- ◆ the sharing of Lennie and George's dream with Crooks
- ◆ Lennie with Curley's wife
- ◆ Lennie and George in the brush at the end.

Themes and ideas:

Think about as wide a range of material as you can, where you could write interestingly about each of the following:

- ◆ dreams (and the American Dream)
- ◆ disappointments
- ◆ failure
- ◆ the outsider
- ◆ the life of the migrant worker
- ◆ the position and role of women in the society portrayed
- ◆ dependency
- ◆ racism
- ◆ animals
- ◆ death
- ◆ failed lives.

Language:

- ◆ different people's speech
- ◆ the uses of description
- ◆ symbolism
- ◆ how the relationship between George and Lennie is shown
- ◆ the effect, effectiveness, and significance of the title
- ◆ how the language creates feelings in the readers
- ◆ the significance of animals and animal imagery in the novel.

Structure:

- ◆ the effect of the order of events
- ◆ the sequence of the brush – the bunkhouse – the ranch – the brush
- ◆ the pace of the story
- ◆ climaxes you can find
- ◆ the building of tension
- ◆ turning points you can find
- ◆ the ways one situation reminds you of others
- ◆ similarities and differences between the opening of the novel and the ending.

Lord of the Flies

Characters, characters' roles, and their relationships:

- ◆ Ralph (and his role as leader)
- ◆ Jack (and his role as leader)
- ◆ the comparisons and contrasts drawn between Ralph and Jack
- ◆ Piggy
- ◆ Simon

- the minor characters (Samneric, Maurice, Percival Wemys Madison, Roger)
- the Naval Officer
- the littluns as a group
- the hunters as a group.

Key events:

Ask yourself what each of the following key events shows you about:
- the characters, their relationships, and attitudes
- the fears and priorities on the island
- the gradual descent into savagery
- the struggle between the opposing powers (of Ralph and Jack)
- themes and ideas important to the novel as a whole
- the writer's methods of influencing what you think and feel
- the writer's uses of language which make you think and feel what you do
- the nature of society on the island
- why you think the event comes at the stage of the novel it does
- what you think the writer's purposes are in including this event.

Here are some key events which are useful for you to look at in detail, and where you should consider the points above:
- the opening description of the boys
- the initial exploration of the island
- the use of the conch
- Jack's breaking of the 'rules'
- killing the pig
- Simon's isolation and death
- tending and neglecting the fire
- the final hunt
- the 'rescue'.

Themes and ideas:

Think about as wide a range of material as you can, where you could write interestingly about each of the following:
- the descent into savagery
- civilization and democracy
- the nature of the beast
- fears
- the role of a leader
- the nature of childhood
- the change from innocence to experience
- faith and belief
- death.

Language:

- symbolism (e.g. the island, the fire, the conch, the beast)
- the changing nature of the boys' speech
- the uses of description
- imagery
- how the changes in the boys are shown individually and collectively.

Structure:

- the effect of the order of events
- the pace of the story
- climaxes you can find
- any turning points you can find
- the significance of the chapter titles
- the way one situation reminds you of another
- the effects of and expectations set up by the opening
- the effects of the ending.

A Kestrel for a Knave

Characters, characters' roles, and relationships:

- Billy (and his relationships with his mother, father, Jud, his teachers, Kes)
- Mrs Casper (and her relationships with Billy, Jud, her husband, her boyfriends)
- the teachers (and their relationships with Billy, other boys)
- what minor characters reveal (e.g. Mr Porter, the farmer, the librarian, Mr Gryce, the Youth Employment Officer).

Key events:

Ask yourself what each of the following key events shows you about:
- Billy's ideas, thoughts and feelings
- Billy's hopes and attitudes
- themes and ideas important to the novel as a whole
- the writer's methods of influencing what you think and feel
- the writer's uses of language which make you think and feel what you do
- the nature of the society Barry Hines is writing about
- why you think the event comes at the stage of the novel it does
- what you think the writer's purposes are in including this event.

Here are some key events which are useful for you to look at in detail, and where you should consider the points above:
- the opening section with Billy and Jud
- Billy's paper round
- the description of the fields
- Billy's acquisition of Kes
- Billy's daydreams in school
- Mr Gryce and the smokers
- the English lesson with Mr Farthing
- Billy's 'tall story'
- the football match
- the changing room and Mr Sugden
- the training of Kes
- Jud's revenge on Billy
- the death of Kes
- Billy in the cinema.

Themes and ideas:

Think about as wide a range of material as you can, where you could write interestingly about each of the following:

- growing up
- isolation and loneliness
- Billy's hopes and aspirations
- education
- social justice
- bullying
- family life and relationships
- nature
- relationships between adults and children
- the nature of children.

Language:

- the uses of different kinds of speech for different characters
- the uses of description
- the weather
- symbols (e.g. Kes, the pit)
- how Billy's feelings are shown.

Structure:

- the effect of the order of events
- the pace of the story
- climaxes you can find
- turning points you can find
- the ways one situation reminds you of another
- the mixture of reality and daydreams
- the mixture of Billy experiencing things and remembering things
- why the novel starts as it does
- why the novel ends as it does
- how the cinema episode recalls a range of events.

The Catcher in the Rye

Characters, characters' roles, and relationships:

- Holden's relationships with:
  - Phoebe
  - Allie
  - his parents
  - Mr Antolini
  - Ackley
  - Stradlater
  - Mr Spencer
  - Lillian Simmons
  - Sally Heyes
  - Jane Gallagher.

Key events:

Ask yourself what each of the following key events shows you about:
- Holden's state of mind
- Holden's thoughts, feelings, and attitudes
- Holden's likes and dislikes
- the ways Holden expresses himself
- themes and ideas important to the novel as a whole
- the writer's methods of influencing what you think and feel
- the writer's uses of language which make you think and feel what you do
- the nature of school or family or New York society
- why you think the event comes at the stage of the novel it does
- what you think the writer's purposes are in including this event.

Here are some key events which are useful for you to look at in detail, and where you should consider the points above:
- what happens in Holden's room at school
- the meeting with Mr Spencer
- leaving Pencey
- meeting Mrs Morrow on the train
- the scene in the Lavender room
- meeting the nuns
- meeting the prostitute, Sunny
- the trip to the skating rink
- the trip to the theatre
- meeting Carl Luce
- the scene in the park at night
- journeys (on the train, in taxis)
- the conversation with Phoebe in their home
- with Phoebe at the art gallery and at the zoo.

Themes and ideas:

Think about as wide a range of material as you can, where you could write interestingly about the following:
- adolescence
- growing up
- the role of family
- loneliness
- knowing yourself
- the nature of New York society
- relationships between adolescents and adults
- love
- dreams and aspirations
- Holden's likes, dislikes, hopes
- religion
- journeys and escape
- the choice and significance of the title.

Language:

- how the first-person narrative is used
- different people's speech

- the effect of description
- symbolism (the broken record, the suitcases, alcohol)
- the ways the reader is directly addressed.

Structure:

- why it is so long before we learn the speaker's name
- the effect of school – New York – home
- the way the novel begins
- the effect of the surprise of the ending
- the effect of so many episodes
- the order the events are told in.

I'm the King of the Castle

Characters, characters' roles, and relationships:

- Kingshaw and Hooper
- Kingshaw and Fielding
- Mr Hooper and Mrs Kingshaw
- Kingshaw and his mother
- Hooper and his father
- what minor characters reveal (Mrs Boland, Miss Mellitt).

Key events:

Ask yourself what each of the following key events show you about:
- the characters, their relationships, and attitudes
- Kingshaw's growing fear and isolation
- themes and ideas important to the novel as a whole
- the writer's methods of influencing what you think and feel
- the writer's uses of language which make you think and feel what you do
- why you think the event comes at the stage of the novel it does
- what you think the writer's purposes are in including this event.

Here are some key events which are useful for you to look at in detail, and where you should consider the points above:
- Mr Hooper and Edmund at the beginning
- Kingshaw's arrival at Warings
- Kingshaw and the crow
- the red room
- in Hang Wood
- Hooper's injury in Hang Wood
- in the shed
- at Leydell Castle
- reactions to Hooper's fall
- Kingshaw in church
- Kingshaw with Fielding
- Kingshaw at Fielding's farm
- Hooper, Kingshaw, and Fielding at Warings
- the ending.

Themes and ideas:

Think about as wide a range of material as you can, where you could write interestingly about each of the following:

- bullying
- parenthood
- relationships between parents and children
- broken families
- functional and dysfunctional families
- isolation
- death and dead creatures
- animals
- fear
- the significance of the title.

Language:

- the ways the children speak
- the ways the adults speak
- how different points of view are shown
- descriptions (rooms, nature, animals, people)
- contrast between nature outside and Warings inside
- some links between what happens outside and inside
- symbols (animals, crow, moth, battle plans, weather, moonlight).

Structure:

- why the novel opens with Hooper and his father
- the effect of the order of events
- the pace of the story
- the uses of flashbacks
- climaxes you can find
- turning points you can find
- how tension is gradually built up
- the ways one situation reminds you of another
- how the novel ends
- why you think the novel ends as it does.

Green Days by the River

Characters, characters' roles, and relationships:

Shell's relationships with:

- Mr Gidharee
- Rosalie
- Joan
- Joe, Lennard, and Freddy
- his mother
- his father
- the dogs
- nature and the land.

Key events:

Ask yourself what each of the following key events shows you about:
- the characters, their relationships, and attitudes
- Shell's increasing understanding and maturity
- themes and ideas important to the novel as a whole
- the writer's methods of influencing what you think and feel
- the writer's uses of language which make you think and feel what you do
- why you think the event comes at the stage of the novel that it does
- what you think the writer's purposes are in including this event.

Here are some key events which are useful for you to look at in detail, and where you should consider the points above:
- Shell's first meeting with Mr Gidharee
- pelting cashews
- Shell's first visit to Cedar Grove
- Discovery Day
- Shell's second visit to Cedar Grove (Chapter 9)
- visit to Port-of-Spain
- with Joan in Sangre-Grande
- encounter with Sonia
- Shell's third visit to Cedar Grove (Chapter 18)
- Christmas day
- getting drunk with Joe, Lennard, and Freddy
- Joan's visit
- praying with mother and father
- Shell and the dogs
- responses to Shell's father's death
- Shell's second visit to Port-of-Spain
- the ending.

Themes and ideas:

Think about as wide a range of material as you can, where you could write interestingly about each of the following:
- growing up
- adolescence
- relationships between parents and children
- threats and violence
- the importance of family
- death
- Shell's four visits to Cedar Grove
- the role of women in the society depicted
- the importance of land
- friendship
- loyalty
- Shell's father and Mr Gidharee as role models
- love, 'real trouble' and marriage.

Language:

- the effects of the first-person narrative
- different uses of speech
- uses of dialect and dialect words
- symbolism (e.g. the dogs, cashews, planting seeds, dragon's blood)
- descriptions of nature
- what Shell hints at but doesn't tell the reader, and the effects of this
- what Shell doesn't tell the reader.

Structure:

- the effect of the order of events
- the pace of the story
- climaxes you can find
- turning points you can find
- the four visits to Cedar Grove
- the two visits to Port-of-Spain
- the ways one situation reminds you of another
- ideas, thoughts, and feelings established in the opening chapter
- why you think the writer chose to end the novel as he did.

Heroes

Characters, characters' roles, and relationships:

- what Francis reveals about himself
- Francis's thoughts, feelings, and attitudes
- Francis and Larry
- Francis and Nicole
- Larry and Nicole
- what minor characters reveal (e.g. Mrs Bellander, Marie LaCroix, Arthur Rivier, Sister Mathilde).

Key events:

Ask yourself what each of the following key events shows you about:
- Larry's thoughts and feelings
- the nature of heroism
- admiration, affection, respect, love
- relationships between the characters
- Francis before and after the war
- themes and ideas important to the novel as a whole
- the writer's methods of influencing what you think and feel
- the writer's uses of language which make you think and feel what you do
- the effects of war
- why you think the event comes at the stage of the novel that it does
- what you think the writer's purposes are in including this event.

Here are some key events which are useful for you to look at in detail, and where you should consider the points above:
- Francis's arrival at Mrs Bellander's
- memories of war
- St Jude Club

- memories of the Wreck Centre
- the table tennis competition
- the match between Francis and Larry
- Larry's return from war
- what happens to Nicole and how she responds to Francis
- in the confessional
- visiting Larry after the war
- the visit to the convent
- the meeting between Francis and Nicole
- the ending.

Themes and ideas:

Think about as wide a range of material as you can, where you could write interestingly about each of the following:

- heroism
- love and affection
- the effects of war
- revenge
- ways in which characters mature
- deformity
- appearance and reality.

Language:

- characters' speech
- the uses of first-person narrative
- the uses and effectiveness of flashbacks
- the use of bold italics
- the uses of description
- methods of building up suspense
- symbols (e.g. guns, table tennis, the scarf)
- how changes in the characters are shown.

Structure:

- the uses of flashbacks
- contrasts between the past and present
- the effect of the order in which events are told
- the pace of the story
- climaxes you can find
- building and dropping of tension
- turning points you can find
- the ways one situation reminds you of another
- why you think the novel begins in the way it does
- why you think the novel ends in the way it does.

Preparing for your examination

You have an hour for this task in the examination, but you are expected to spend ten minutes planning your answer before you begin to write. Failure to do so properly can make a big difference to your grade.

You must answer **one** question out of a choice of **three**.

You will always have to answer on two pre-1914 poems, and you will have to answer on the pair of post-1914 poets you have studied – that is, either Duffy and Armitage or Clarke and Heaney.

You will always be asked to compare, so it is important when you are revising to make sure that you look at the poems in pairs and in groups to prepare for this. Don't revise them separately, one after another.

The comparison in the exam may take different forms. The question might be like one of the following:

◆ A question that asks you to compare the ways Clarke and Heaney (or Duffy and Armitage), as well as two pre-1914 poets, present some topic. This involves comparing the four poems.

◆ A question that is divided into two parts, which asks you to compare
(a) one Clarke with one Heaney (or one Duffy with one Armitage) poem
(b) two pre-1914 poems.
This involves comparing two poems in the first part and two in the second.

◆ A question which asks you to compare
(a) one post-1914 poem with one pre-1914 poem
(b) another post-1914 poem with another pre-1914 poem.

Government rules mean that at least one poem must be named in each question. Some questions may name more than one poem. But the poems that are mostly likely to be named in the questions are the **Key Poems**.

The lists of Key Poems for Foundation and for Higher tiers are slightly different, so it is important to know which tier you will be sitting. This is the only part of your English and English Literature revision where the tier you are sitting makes any difference.

Here is the list of Key Poems.

Foundation		
Duffy	**Armitage**	**Pre-1914 bank**
Stealing	My father thought it	The Man He Killed
Salome	November	The Song of the Old Mother
Education for Leisure	Kid	On My First Sonne
Havisham	Hitcher	The Laboratory

Heaney	Clarke	Pre-1914 bank
Mid-Term Break	Baby-sitting	The Eagle
Follower	On the Train	The Song of the Old Mother
Digging	Catrin	On My First Sonne
Death of a Naturalist	The Field-Mouse	Sonnet: I love to see the summer

Higher		
Duffy	**Armitage**	**Pre-1914 bank**
Anne Hathaway	Mother, any distance	Sonnet: My mistress' eyes
Before You Were Mine	Homecoming	My Last Duchess
Education for Leisure	Kid	On My First Sonne
Havisham	Hitcher	The Laboratory

Heaney	Clarke	Pre-1914 bank
At a Potato Digging	Cold Knap Lake	Patrolling Barnegat
Storm on the Island	A Difficult Birth	The Affliction of Margaret
Digging	Catrin	On My First Sonne
Death of a Naturalist	The Field-Mouse	Sonnet: I love to see the summer

There may be more poems named in the question in the Foundation paper than there are in the Higher paper. This is to help those doing the Foundation paper to write about the poems they are likely to know best, and to enable Higher candidates to choose whichever poems they like (in addition to the named poem or poems) from those that suit the needs of the question.

Remember! Because each question has to name at least one of these poems, your first task in revision is to get to know them very well and to find plenty of points of similarity and difference between them.

Sometimes a question might ask you to choose poems to write about from a list. In this case there will always be poems from the Key Poems list so you could perfectly well answer the question from those, but there may be some additional poems named in the list. If you felt most confident writing about those other poems, then you would be able to do so.

Let me give you an example.

Question

Compare the methods the writers use to create a character for the speaker of the poems. You need to compare two poems from List A with two poems from List B:

List A	List B
Stealing (Key F)	The Man He Killed (Key F)
Anne Hathaway (Key H)	The Laboratory (Key F and H)
Elvis's Twin Sister	Ulysses
Hitcher (Key F and H)	My Last Duchess (Key H)
Those bastards in their mansions	The Affliction of Margaret (Key H)

You could write about the Key Poems if you wanted to, or you could equally well write about others in the list. The choice would be yours.

Using this *Revision Guide*

The next part of this *Revision Guide* is divided into two parts according to what you have been studying:

◆ **Section 1:** Clarke, Heaney, pre-1914 bank
◆ **Section 2:** Duffy, Armitage, pre-1914 bank

Use the part of the guide that handles the post-1914 poets you have been studying.

Whichever section you work on, first remind yourself of the Assessment Objectives that are tested in this part of the exam paper. The lists of features of poems, which you should think about while you are revising, are built on these.

> ❏ Respond to texts critically, sensitively, and in detail, selecting appropriate ways to convey your response, using textual evidence as appropriate.
> ❏ Explore how language, structure, and forms contribute to the meanings of texts, considering different approaches to texts and alternative interpretations.
> ❏ Explore relationships and comparisons between texts, selecting and evaluating relevant material.

Note *Look back to pages 6–7 where I broke down these Assessment Objectives for you, showing you what kinds of things you might write about.*

Whether you choose to work on Section 1 or Section 2 below, the structure is the same:

1 Key Poems common to both tiers
2 Other Key Poems for Foundation
3 Other Key Poems for Higher.

In order to encourage you think in terms of comparison, each of these three sections covers six poems. And the lists of what to think about are designed in the same way, so that it should be easy for you to find areas to compare.

These groups are not fixed in any way. You need to be able to compare any poem you have studied with any other poem. These groups are organized merely for convenience to help you work through your revision material.

Heaney, Clarke, and Pre-1914 Poetry Bank
Key Poems: Foundation and Higher

Heaney: 'Digging'

◆ effect of opening sentence	◆ uses of description
◆ speaker's feelings/attitudes	◆ uses of alliteration
◆ uses of language	◆ uses of assonance
◆ effect of lines ending where they do	◆ use of metaphors
◆ variety of syntax	◆ use of extended metaphor
◆ use of minor sentences	◆ use of similes
◆ presentation of feelings	◆ use of images
◆ rural setting	◆ use of one rhyme
◆ nature	◆ use of stanzas of irregular length
◆ relationships	◆ link between opening and ending
◆ father and son	◆ the turning point
◆ the generations	◆ effect of title
◆ family	◆ effect of final stanza
◆ writing	◆ your feelings about the speaker
◆ work	◆ your feelings about his father
◆ cycles of nature	◆ your feelings about the way the
◆ storytelling	situation is presented.

Clarke: 'Catrin'

◆ effect of opening line	◆ families
◆ speaker's feelings and attitudes	◆ uses of description
◆ the language the speaker uses	◆ effects of alliteration
◆ repetition	◆ use of metaphors
◆ patterning of sentences	◆ use of images
◆ effect of lines ending where they do	◆ linked metaphors (the rope)
◆ effects of syntactical inversion	◆ effect of two stanzas
◆ variety of syntax	◆ effect of stanzas of uneven length
◆ presentation of feelings	◆ what is implied, not stated
◆ empathy with others	◆ use of adjectives
◆ memories	◆ use of present participles (words ending in -ing)
◆ relationship between mother and daughter	◆ ambiguities
◆ birth	◆ effects/meanings of ending
◆ becoming separate	◆ speaker's point of view
◆ struggles	◆ your feelings about the speaker
◆ storytelling	◆ your feelings about Catrin
◆ use of ordinary experience	◆ your feelings about the way the memories are presented.

Ben Jonson: 'On My First Sonne'

- effect of opening line
- speaker's feelings/attitudes
- uses of language
- presentation of feelings
- relationships
- death
- father and son
- families
- mourning
- writing
- effect of rhetorical questions
- effect of exclamations
- effect of money imagery ('lent', 'pay')
- effect of lack of stanza breaks
- effect of the rhymes
- effect of iambic pentameter lines
- effect of rhyming couplets
- ambiguity of 'O could I loose all father, now'
- any other ambiguities
- effect of choice of title
- your feelings about the speaker
- your feelings about the way the situation is presented.

Heaney: 'Death of a Naturalist'

- effect of opening
- speaker's feelings/attitudes
- uses of language
- effect of lines ending where they do
- use of threatening/unexpected words
- variety of syntax
- presentation of feelings
- rural setting
- memory
- nature
- threats
- reflection/meditation
- people and nature
- storytelling
- innocence and experience
- uses of senses
- uses of description
- uses of alliteration and assonance
- use of irregular iambic pentameter
- use of part-rhyme
- effect of two stanzas of uneven length
- effect of title
- effect of last sentence
- your feelings about the speaker
- your feelings about the ways the situation is presented.

Clarke: 'The Field-Mouse'

- effect of opening line
- speaker's feelings/attitudes
- the language used
- surprising/dramatic words and phrases
- effect of lines ending the way they do
- variety of syntax
- variety of vocabulary
- presentation of feelings
- empathy with others
- cycles of nature
- war
- death
- struggles
- rural setting
- people and nature
- mortality
- reflection/meditation
- storytelling
- use of description
- use of metaphors
- extended metaphor
- use of images
- use of comparison
- effect of three nine-line stanzas
- what is implied, not stated
- movement from impersonal to personal
- shifts from general to particular
- use of political/war references
- ambiguities and multiple meanings
- political implications
- effects/meanings of ending
- your feelings about the speaker
- your feelings about the ending
- your feelings about the way the situation is presented.

John Clare: Sonnet: 'I love to see the summer'

◆ effect of opening line	◆ use of sonnet form
◆ speaker's feelings/attitudes	◆ effect of lack of stanzas
◆ uses of language	◆ effect of rhyming couplets
◆ uses of syntax	◆ effect of iambic pentameter lines
◆ syntactical inversion	◆ effect of lack of punctuation
◆ nature	◆ effect of ending
◆ people and nature	◆ your feelings about the speaker
◆ uses of description	◆ your feelings about the way
◆ effects of alliteration	nature is presented.

Other Key Poems: Foundation

Heaney: 'Mid-Term Break'

◆ effect of opening sentence	◆ memory
◆ speaker's feelings/attitudes	◆ storytelling
◆ uses of language	◆ uses of description
◆ effect of lines ending where they do	◆ use of alliteration
◆ variety of syntax	◆ use of metaphors
◆ use of minor sentences	◆ use of images
◆ presentation of feelings	◆ use of irregular pentameter
◆ families	◆ use of seven three-line stanzas
◆ relationships	◆ effect of single line at the end
◆ death	◆ the turning point
◆ relationship between fathers and sons	◆ effect of title
◆ innocence and experience	◆ your feelings about the speaker
	◆ your feelings about the way the situation is presented.

Clarke: 'Baby-sitting'

◆ effect of opening line	◆ struggles
◆ speaker's feelings/attitudes	◆ uses of description
◆ the language the speaker uses	◆ effects of alliteration
◆ surprising/dramatic phrases	◆ use of metaphors
◆ effect of lines ending where they do	◆ use of images
◆ variety of syntax	◆ use of comparisons
◆ presentation of feelings	◆ effect of two stanzas
◆ empathy with others	◆ effect of balanced stanzas
◆ memories	◆ what is implied, not stated
◆ relationship between adults and children	◆ use of adjectives
◆ reflection/meditation	◆ ambiguities
◆ families	◆ effects/meanings of ending
◆ storytelling	◆ your feelings about the speaker
◆ use of ordinary experiences	◆ your feelings about the baby
	◆ your feelings about the way the situation is presented.

W. B. Yeats: 'Song of the Old Mother'

- effect of opening line
- speaker's feelings/attitudes
- uses of language
- presentation of feelings
- contrast between age and youth
- generations
- work
- reflection/meditation
- innocence and experience
- struggle
- effect of use of lists
- effect of pentameter lines
- effect of rhyming couplets
- effect of alliteration
- parallel between first two and last two lines
- significance of the title – why 'Song'?
- your feelings about the speaker
- your feelings about the way the situation is presented.

Heaney: 'Follower'

- effect of opening sentence
- speaker's feelings/attitudes
- uses of language
- effect of lines ending where they do
- variety of syntax
- use of minor sentence
- presentation of feelings
- rural setting
- work
- relationships
- relationship between fathers and sons
- the generations
- families
- reflection/meditation
- cycles of nature
- uses of description
- uses of simile
- effects of alliteration
- use of images
- use of six four-line stanzas
- effects of rhyme
- use of basically regular, eight-syllable line
- contrast between opening and ending
- the turning point
- effect of title
- effect of final sentence
- your feelings about the speaker
- your feelings about his father
- your feelings about the way the situation is presented.

Clarke: 'On the Train'

- effect of opening sentence
- speaker's feelings/attitudes
- the language used
- surprising/dramatic phrases
- building of tension
- uses of repetition
- effect of lines ending where they do
- variety of syntax
- use of minor sentences
- presentation of feelings
- creation of different voices
- empathy with others
- journeys
- death
- struggles
- relationships
- use of ordinary experience
- families
- social attitudes/values
- reflection/meditation
- uses of description
- uses of metaphors
- use of images
- effect of four six-line stanzas
- what is implied, not stated
- ambiguities
- effects/meanings of ending
- your feelings about the speaker
- your feelings about the ending
- your feelings about the way the situation is presented.

Alfred Tennyson: 'The Eagle'	
◆ effect of opening line	◆ effect of rhymes
◆ feelings/attitudes	◆ uses of description
◆ uses of language	◆ effect of alliteration
◆ presentation of feelings	◆ effect of two regular stanzas
◆ nature	◆ effect of regular, eight-syllable iambic lines
◆ threat	◆ your feelings about the eagle
◆ use of adjectives	◆ your feelings about the way the situation is presented.
◆ use of personification	
◆ use of simile	

Other Key Poems: Higher

Heaney: 'At a Potato Digging'	
◆ effect of opening line	◆ effects of similes
◆ speaker's feelings/attitudes	◆ effects of alliteration
◆ uses of language	◆ use of metaphors
◆ effect of lines ending where they do	◆ use of four-line stanzas
◆ variety of syntax	◆ effect of seven- and six-line stanzas in II
◆ nature	◆ political suggestions
◆ work	◆ effect of three sections
◆ fear	◆ your feelings about the speaker
◆ birth and death	◆ your feelings about the way the situation is presented.
◆ cycles of nature/history	
◆ reflection/meditation	
◆ use of lists	

Clarke: 'A Difficult Birth'	
◆ effect of opening two lines	◆ uses of metaphors
◆ speaker's feelings/attitudes	◆ extended metaphor
◆ the language the speaker uses	◆ uses of images
◆ surprising/dramatic phrases	◆ use of comparisons
◆ effect of lines ending where they do	◆ effect of four six-line stanzas
◆ variety of syntax	◆ what is implied, not stated
◆ variety of vocabulary	◆ use of religious references
◆ effect of minor sentences	◆ ambiguities
◆ presentation of feelings	◆ multiple meanings
◆ empathy with others	◆ political implications
◆ birth	◆ effects/meanings of ending
◆ struggles	◆ your feelings about the speaker
◆ rural setting	◆ your feelings about the ending
◆ storytelling	◆ your feelings about the way the situation is presented.
◆ reflection/meditation	
◆ uses of description	

William Wordsworth: 'The Affliction of Margaret'

- effect of opening line
- speaker's feelings/attitudes
- uses of language
- creation of voices
- use of exclamations
- presentation of feelings
- relationships
- families
- loss
- mother/son
- mourning/separation
- innocence and experience
- storytelling
- reflection/meditation
- use of lists
- use of metaphors
- use of eight-syllable iambic lines
- effect of regular stanzas
- use of rhymes
- ambiguity
- possible political/social implications
- effect of final line
- effect of title
- your feelings about the mother
- your feelings about the son
- your feelings about society
- your feelings about the way the situation is presented.

Heaney: 'Storm on the Island'

- effect of opening two lines
- speaker's feelings/attitudes
- uses of language
- effects of lines ending where they do
- use of dramatic words
- methods of involving reader
- effect of using present tense
- variety of syntax
- presentation of feelings
- rural setting
- violence
- threat
- fear
- people and nature
- innocence and experience
- uses of sound and sight
- uses of description
- uses of metaphor
- use of images
- uses of paradox (e.g. 'exploding comfortably')
- metaphors of war
- effect of half-rhyme at end
- effect of lack of stanza breaks
- what is implied, not stated
- effect of last line
- your feelings about the speaker
- your feelings about the way the situation is presented.

Clarke: 'Cold Knap Lake'

- effect of opening
- speaker's feelings/attitudes
- the language used
- surprising/dramatic phrases
- building of tension
- effect of lines ending where they do
- effects of syntactical inversion
- presentation of feelings
- empathy with others
- reflection/meditation
- death
- struggles
- relationships
- adults and children
- families
- people and nature
- reflection on memory
- social attitudes/values
- uses of colour
- uses of description
- use of images
- effect of five stanzas
- what is implied, not stated
- ambiguities
- effects of questions
- effect of full rhyme at the end
- effects/meanings of final couplet
- your feelings about the speaker
- your feelings about the other characters
- your feelings about the way the situation is presented.

Walt Whitman: 'Patrolling Barnegat'

- effect of opening line
- feelings/attitudes
- uses of language
- nature
- people and nature
- struggle
- work
- threat
- use of adjectives
- uses of description
- effects of alliteration
- use of modified sonnet form
- effect of use of present participles (words ending in -ing)
- use of parallel structures
- effect of only one sentence
- effect of title
- possible meanings of last line
- your feelings about the way the situation is presented.

Duffy, Armitage, and Pre-1914 Poetry Bank
Key Poems: Foundation and Higher

Duffy: 'Education for Leisure'

◆ who the speaker is	◆ what is implied, not stated
◆ what he/she is like	◆ persona's view of the world
◆ his/her attitudes and values	◆ persona's motivations
◆ the language the speaker uses	◆ effect of regular stanzas
◆ simple, clipped sentences	◆ how each stanza begins
◆ staccato statements	◆ sequence of the stanzas
◆ irony of 'I am a genius'	◆ effect of lack of rhyme
◆ irony of 'I see that it is good'	◆ Duffy's attitudes
◆ other ironies	◆ Duffy's point of view
◆ discontent	◆ social comment
◆ boredom	◆ implied political comment
◆ delinquency	◆ meanings of title
◆ violence	◆ your feelings about the speaker
◆ death	◆ your feelings about the way the
◆ threats	situation is presented.

Armitage: 'Hitcher'

◆ who the speaker is	◆ what is implied, not stated
◆ what he/she is like	◆ persona's view of the world
◆ his/her attitudes and values	◆ persona's motivations
◆ the language the speaker uses	◆ effect of the regular stanzas
◆ source in newspaper reports	◆ how each stanza begins
◆ effects of different kinds of language	◆ sequence of the stanzas
◆ creation of different voices	◆ effect of the rhymes/half-rhymes
◆ similarities/differences between speaker and hitcher and how they are shown	◆ Armitage's point of view
	◆ social comment
◆ use of simple and compound sentences	◆ why this choice of title
◆ relationships	◆ your feelings about the speaker
◆ violence	◆ your feelings about the hitcher
◆ psychopathic behaviour	◆ your feelings about the way the situation is presented.

Ben Jonson: 'On My First Sonne'

◆ who the speaker is	◆ effect of the rhyming couplets
◆ what he is like	◆ sequence of the couplets
◆ his attitudes, values, beliefs	◆ effect of full stop in line 5
◆ the language the speaker uses	◆ ambiguity of 'O, could I loose all
◆ effect of exclamations	father, now'
◆ effect of rhetorical questions	◆ any other ambiguities
◆ effect of money imagery ('lent', 'pay')	◆ effect of the rhymes
◆ relationships	◆ possible meanings of the final couplet
◆ death and mourning	◆ effect of choice of title
◆ faith and belief	◆ your feelings about the speaker
◆ what is implied, not stated	◆ your feelings about the way the
◆ speaker's view of the world	situation is presented.

Duffy: 'Havisham'

◆ who the speaker is	◆ what is implied, not stated
◆ what she is like	◆ persona's view of the world
◆ her attitudes and values	◆ persona's motivations
◆ the language the persona uses	◆ effect of breaking the stanzas by
◆ source in Dickens's *Great Expectations*	enjambment
◆ effect of different kinds of sentences	◆ how each stanza begins
◆ onomatopoeia	◆ sequence of the stanzas
◆ use of colours	◆ effect of lack of rhyme
◆ effect of stuttering	◆ effect of hint of half-rhyme at end
◆ use of oxymoron 'love's hate'	('cake'/'breaks')
◆ broken syntax/rhythm/lines	◆ Duffy's point of view
◆ discontent	◆ social comment
◆ love and hate	◆ why the title 'Havisham', not
◆ relationships	'Miss Havisham'
◆ violence (feelings/vocabulary)	◆ your feelings about the speaker
◆ death	◆ your feelings about the way the
◆ threats	situation is presented.

Armitage: 'Kid'

◆ who the speaker is	◆ power over others
◆ what he is like	◆ Robin's view of the world
◆ his attitudes and values	◆ range of images
◆ playing with language	◆ effect of having no stanzas
◆ source in *Batman*	◆ change from 'big shot' to
◆ *Batman* details and references	'you baby'
◆ uses of Americanisms	◆ sequence of the statements
◆ Robin's attitude to Batman and	◆ effect of the rhymes/half-rhymes
how it is shown	◆ Armitage's point of view
◆ making jokes out of *Batman* clichés	◆ effect of choice of title
◆ relationships	◆ your feelings about the speaker
◆ growing up	◆ your feelings about the way the
◆ adolescence	situation is presented.

Robert Browning: 'The Laboratory'	
◆ who the speaker is	◆ what is implied, not stated
◆ what she is like	◆ persona's view of the world
◆ her attitudes and values	◆ how tension and suspense are
◆ the language the persona uses	created
◆ effects of colours, taste, other senses	◆ effect of regular stanzas/rhymes
◆ effects of imagery	◆ sequence of the stanzas
◆ effects of questions	◆ how mystery is created
◆ effects of exclamations	◆ meanings and effects of last stanza
◆ how the situation is made dramatic	◆ effect of choice of title
◆ relationships	◆ speaker's point of view
◆ death	◆ poet's possible point of view
◆ murder	◆ your feelings about the speaker
◆ violence	◆ your feelings about the way the
◆ threats	situation is presented.

Other Key Poems: Foundation

Duffy: 'Stealing'	
◆ who the speaker is	◆ the persona's view of the world
◆ what he/she is like	◆ the persona's motivations
◆ his/her attitudes and values	◆ who the persona might be speaking to
◆ the language the persona uses	◆ effect of the regular stanzas
◆ what he/she steals and why	◆ how each stanza begins
◆ simple sentences	◆ sequence of the stanzas
◆ minor sentences	◆ possible meanings of the last line
◆ how the speaker's feelings are shown	◆ effect of lack of rhyme
◆ effect of colloquial language	◆ Duffy's ideas, point of view
◆ discontent	◆ social comment
◆ boredom	◆ implied political comment
◆ delinquency	◆ significance of the title
◆ violence	◆ your feelings about the speaker
◆ threats	◆ your feelings about the way the
◆ what is implied rather than stated	situation is presented.

Armitage: 'My father thought it'

◆ who the speaker is	◆ effect of rhymes and pattern of rhymes
◆ what he is like	
◆ the description of the ear-piercing	◆ effect of the irregular stanzas
◆ the language the speaker uses	◆ how each stanza begins
◆ how different voices are created	◆ sequence of the stanzas
◆ attitudes and values of speaker	◆ use of a modified sonnet form
◆ attitudes and values of father	◆ effect of the opening line
◆ change	◆ use of possible pun
◆ growing up	◆ effect of italics at the end
◆ relationships	◆ significance of the title
◆ conflict between generations	◆ your feelings about the speaker
◆ images of 'wept', 'like a tear'	◆ your feelings about the father
◆ what is implied rather than stated	◆ your feelings about how the situation is presented.
◆ use of similes	

Thomas Hardy: 'The Man He Killed'

◆ who the speaker is	◆ what is implied rather than stated
◆ what he is like	◆ use of clipped phrases/sentences
◆ his attitudes and values	◆ speaker's view of the world
◆ the language the speaker uses	◆ effect of regular rhymes
◆ effect of the use of direct speech	◆ social comment
◆ effect of the use of slang	◆ political comment
◆ meditation on an event	◆ possible ideas/viewpoint of the writer
◆ war	
◆ friendship	◆ significance of the title
◆ relationships	◆ your feelings about the speaker
◆ responsibilities	◆ your feelings about the way the situation is presented.
◆ attitudes and values	

Duffy: 'Salome'

- who the speaker is
- what she is like
- her attitudes and values
- the language the persona uses
- source in Bible story
- changes from the Bible story
- varied colloquial language
- sensual description
- effect of use of slang
- how the persona's feelings are shown
- discontent
- boredom

- violence
- psychopathic behaviour
- what is implied rather than stated
- the persona's view of the world
- the persona's motivations
- effect of the irregular stanzas
- how each stanza begins
- sequence of the stanzas
- effect of rhymes and half-rhymes
- effect of choice of free verse
- your feelings about the speaker
- your feelings about the way the situation is presented.

Armitage: 'November'

- who the speaker is
- who the other characters are
- what the speaker is like
- who you think 'you' is and why
- the repetition of personal pronouns (we, you, she)
- the speaker's attitudes and values
- the way the grandmother is presented
- relationships
- responsibilities
- attitudes to old people

- relationships between generations
- what is implied rather than stated
- the effect of the regular stanzas
- the effect of the couplet at the end
- the sequence of the stanzas
- the effect of the final couplet
- significance of the title
- your feelings about the speaker
- your feelings about the other characters
- your feelings about the way the situation is presented.

W. B. Yeats: 'Song of the Old Mother'

- who the speaker is
- what she is like
- her attitudes and values
- the language the Old Mother uses
- range of details to show lifestyle
- contrast between age and youth
- meditation on her life
- work
- attitudes to young people
- attitudes to old people
- what is implied rather than stated
- effect of use of lists

- effect of repetition of 'and'
- speaker's view of the world
- effect of rhymes
- parallel between first two and last two lines
- social comment
- possible viewpoint/ideas of the writer
- significance of the title
- why 'Song'?
- your feelings about the old woman
- your feelings about the way the situation is presented.

Other Key Poems: Higher

Duffy: 'Anne Hathaway'

- who the speaker is
- what she is like
- her attitudes and values
- the language the persona uses
- source in Shakespeare's will
- the central conceit of writing/relationship
- how the persona's feelings are shown
- effect of use of lists
- effect of use of series of metaphors
- effect of use of extended metaphor
- effect of alliteration in line 12
- effect of use of literary terms
- love
- relationships
- writing

- possessiveness/being possessed
- husband and wife
- use of sonnet form
- where the sections break
- how the conceit develops
- how the argument develops
- effect of uses of iambic pentameter
- effect of rhyme in final couplet
- Duffy's possible ideas/point of view
- significance of the title (why not Anne Shakespeare?)
- your feelings about the speaker
- your feelings about the relationship as presented in the poem
- your feelings about the way the situation is presented.

Armitage: 'Mother, any distance'

- who the speaker is
- what he is like
- his feelings and attitudes
- the language the persona uses
- how the persona's feelings are shown
- effect of use of lists
- description of taking measurements
- metaphor of measuring house/measuring relationship
- relationships
- mother/son
- growing up
- becoming separate
- the persona's hopes/state of mind
- effect of use of modified sonnet form
- why the three sections
- how the argument develops

- how the thoughts and feelings develop
- sequence of the stanzas
- possible meanings of the last sentence
- metaphors of lines 11–12
- effect of antithesis ('Anchor. Kite'; 'fall or fly')
- effect of use of rhyme
- effect of use of unrhyming lines
- Armitage's possible point of view
- your feelings about the speaker
- your feelings about the mother
- your feelings about the relationship portrayed
- your feelings about the way the situation is presented.

William Shakespeare: Sonnet: 'My mistress' eyes'

- who the speaker is
- what he is like
- his attitudes/likes/dislikes
- the language the persona uses
- what he values/praises his mistress for
- the ways he satirises clichés
- relationships
- love
- satire
- use of the sonnet form

- use of structure: three quatrains and a rhyming couplet
- the sequence of the sections
- the way the argument develops
- the sequence of thought in the poem
- the turning point
- effect of the regular rhyme scheme
- possible meanings of the final couplet
- your own response to the speaker
- your response to the way the situation is presented.

Duffy: 'Before You Were Mine'

- who the speaker is
- what she is like
- her attitudes and values
- the language the persona uses
- effect of reference to Marilyn Monroe
- the idea of writing about times before the speaker was born
- how a picture of the mother is built up
- how the feelings of the persona are shown
- effect of use of snapshot images
- effect of use of ambiguity
- effect of use of alliteration
- effect of use of colloquial language
- love
- relationships

- looking back/memory
- possessiveness
- daughter/mother
- becoming separate
- effect of use of regular stanzas
- how each stanza begins
- sequence of the stanzas
- effect of use of parallel structures
- effect of use of succinct lists
- effect of lack of rhyme
- Duffy's possible ideas, point of view
- significance of the title
- your feelings/ideas about the speaker
- your feelings/ideas about the mother
- your feelings/ideas about the relationship presented.

Armitage: 'Homecoming'

- who the speaker is
- what he is like
- his feelings and memories
- the language the persona uses
- the significance of the opening line
- the way the idea in the first stanza relates to the rest of the poem
- how different voices are created
- extended metaphor of jacket/person fitting
- effect of use of different sentence structures
- relationships
- trust

- parent/child relationships
- love
- adolescent anxieties
- looking back/memory
- effect of irregular stanzas
- four sections
- sequence of the stanzas
- the way line 21 links back to first stanza
- possible meanings of last sentence
- effect of lack of rhyme
- Armitage's possible point of view
- your feelings about the way the situation is presented.

Robert Browning: 'My Last Duchess'

◆ who the speaker is	◆ threat
◆ what the situation is	◆ possible psychopathic behaviour
◆ who the persona is speaking to and why	◆ what is implied rather than stated
◆ the language the speaker uses	◆ persona's view of the world
◆ the variety of syntactical structures	◆ persona's motivations
◆ the way the persona uses references	◆ how mystery is created
◆ effect of the use of images	◆ effects of the dashes
◆ how the situation is made dramatic	◆ effects of inclusion of other voices
◆ the way tension and suspense are built up	◆ how these are created
◆ use of colloquial and formal forms of address	◆ why you think the poem ends as it does
◆ love	◆ effect of choice of title
◆ relationships	◆ poet's possible point of view
◆ violence	◆ your feelings about the speaker
	◆ your feelings about the way the situation is presented.

What you will be tested on

In the **prose** section you will be tested on:

◆ your response to the text(s)
◆ the ways the writers write.

With the short stories, you may also be asked to compare.

In the **poetry** section you will be tested on:

◆ your response to the texts
◆ the ways the poets write
◆ comparison.

Planning effectively

There are several steps to take before you begin to write. This planning time is crucial to your success. Never start to write as soon as you have chosen your question. Always make sure that you use the key words of the task to make a plan.

I am going to take you through the following important stages, with some examples:

❑ finding the key words of the task
❑ using them for a plan
❑ sequencing your points so that they develop into an answer to the question.

Prose

On the Foundation paper all the questions will have bullet points to help you plan. On the Higher paper, only some of the questions will have bullet points.

Here are some examples to show you the difference between a Higher question and a Foundation one:

Higher

Compare the ways the writers show adults behaving towards children in 'Snowdrops' and one other story.

Foundation

Compare the ways the writers show adults behaving towards children in 'Snowdrops' and one other story.

Write about:
◆ how the adults behave towards the children
◆ methods the writers use to show this behaviour
◆ similarities and differences between the behaviour of the adults in the stories towards children and how these are shown.

Key words

These are:
- ✔ compare
- ✔ ways the writers show
- ✔ adults behave towards children
- ✔ 'Snowdrops'
- ✔ one other story.

Choose a story to go with 'Snowdrops' that has adults and children and that you know well. Choose the one about which you have the most things to say.

For this example I'm going to choose 'Superman and Paula Brown's New Snowsuit'.

Planning

Make a list for each story of the adults, and the children their behaviour relates to:

'Snowdrops'		'Superman and Paula Brown's New Snowsuit'	
Adults	**Children**	**Adults**	**Children**
Mother	The boy	Uncle Frank	The speaker
Father	The boy	Mother	The speaker
Miss Webster	The boy The class	Mrs Fein	The speaker
Miss Lewis	The class	Mrs Stirling	David The speaker

You can probably find something to say about each of these, so the next stage is to think about the methods the writers use:

'Snowdrops'	'Superman and Paula Brown's New Snowsuit'
The boy's point of view	The speaker's point of view
Direct speech	Direct speech
The boy overhearing	Adults not listening
The boy misunderstanding	Adults not understanding
Description of Miss Webster	Mother getting rid of the speaker to bed
Adults and children thinking about different things	Adults and children seeing things differently
Boy seeing but not interpreting	At first speaker sees but doesn't interpret; she changes
Dramatic irony of boy not grasping the point about Miss Webster's boyfriend	Dramatic irony of speaker's innocent view of her mother's behaviour
Children's attitudes to adults more evident than adults' attitudes to children	Children's attitudes to adults more evident than adults' attitudes to children
Boy still has innocent view of ways adults behave at end	Speaker disillusioned about ways adults behave at end
Reader has to infer information from naive narrator	Reader has to infer from naive narrator

Having done this, you can see that there are more similarities than differences between the two stories and the methods that the writers use. I would start with this statement as the basis for my essay, and then illustrate it by using the material I have in the lists.

In the essay I would use details from the two texts to support the points I was making about the similarities and differences between the stories - between the ways the adults behave towards the children and between the methods the writers use to show this behaviour.

I've given you an example of the ways in which the question on the Higher and Foundation papers may be very similar. But sometimes they might be different.

Here is an example of a Foundation question on *To Kill a Mockingbird*.

Foundation

How does Harper Lee show Jem changing during the course of the novel?

Write about:
- what he is like at the beginning and the end
- how events in the novel show him changing
- how Harper Lee shows the changes in him.

Key words

These are:
- ✔ Jem
- ✔ changes
- ✔ methods of showing changes.

The bullet points can help you to fill out your plan:

- Jem at the beginning
- Jem at the end
- key events for Jem.

Planning

A useful style of plan here would be a three-column one:

Key events	Jem's changes	Methods
Jem at beginning		Scout's narrative
Influence of mother's death		
Radley house		
Jem taking Scout to school	Responsibility	
Jem at school	Separation from Scout	
Cunninghams	Jem teaching Scout	Conversations
Games with Scout and Dill		Scout's observations Scout's accounts
Jem's moodiness	Adolescence	Scout's reactions
Jem's pants	Growing understanding	
The knot-hole	End of childhood	Conversations with Atticus
Embarrassments	More self-consciousness	Narrative
The fire	People's values	Use of Miss Maudie
Tim Johnson	New view of Atticus	Reactions of others, e.g. Heck Tate
Mrs Dubose	Other people's shoes	Moral tale; symbolism
Jem at twelve	More moods	Calpurnia's explanations to Scout
Black church	Racial difference	Different reactions
Jem withdraws from Scout	Awareness of growing	Scout's observations
The jail	Concern for Atticus	
The trial	Legal justice Moral justice Prejudice	
Dolphus Raymond	Survival	Dolphus's voice
Jem finding out for himself		
End of trial	More complex view	Conversations with Atticus
Jem acting out	Expression of anger at injustice	What Scout tells but doesn't understand
Bob Ewell's death	Maturity	
Meeting Boo	Understanding	Parallel and contrast with beginning of novel

There is far more material here than you would be able to fit into an answer in 45 minutes, but what I have done is list some events, try to link each of them with a stage in Jem's development, and then try to find a different method of presentation for as many as possible of the events. A good answer would probably deal with the beginning, the ending and four or five of the stages in between. You would need to make sure that you refer to details in the text in order to support the points you make.

Higher

Many of the questions which are set in the Higher paper are broader than those on the Foundation Paper. This will allow you to range more widely through the text but also to be make careful choices on what you choose to write about in order to answer the question. The usual pattern on the paper is that one question will have bullet points and the other will not.

Here is an example of a question without bullet points:

> How does Michael Anthony present the difficulties of growing up in *Green Days by the River*?

Key words

These are:

✔ how … present
✔ difficulties of growing up.

The first thing to think about is: Who is seen to be growing up?

◆ Shell
◆ Rosalie
◆ possibly Joan

Next, what are the issues they confront which make growing up difficult? Here are some issues, but I am sure you would be able to think of others of your own. That is fine. You don't have to write about everything you can think of, but there are ways of grouping these ideas together to give shape and direction to your essay.

◆ moving house
◆ parents
◆ poverty
◆ school, or lack of school
◆ role models
◆ relationships

◆ sickness
◆ death
◆ sexual attraction
◆ moral responsibility
◆ social expectations

The other important thing to think about is the 'how'. In order to do this you need to think about form, structure, and language. All of these aspects can be linked with events in the novel which show the difficulties of growing up, and key events which show those difficulties:

◆ use of first-person narrative
◆ different uses of speech
◆ what dialects show
◆ how people modify their speech depending on the situation
◆ symbolism
◆ the four visits to Cedar Grove
◆ relationships between the young people and their elders
◆ parallels/contrasts between Shell's father and Mr Gidharee
◆ comparative/contrasting adult expectations
◆ how travelling shows difficulties
◆ the use of presence and absence of characters
◆ how events remind you of other events.

If you look back to the notes on this novel (page 26) you can see that a lot of the things in the revision list would be useful to you in this essay. Of course you would have to select, and while you were writing the essay you would need to be making links between the difficulties, the key events, and the methods used.

Poetry

There are several different types of comparative questions on poetry and it's useful to practise making plans for these different kinds of question. But in every case, you are still being asked to do the same things:

◆   write on two pre-1914 poems
◆   write on two post-1914 poems
◆   compare poems
◆   show your response to the poems
◆   compare the poets' methods of presentation.

In addition, every question will name at least one of the Key Poems you have studied. Sometimes the question may name more than one.

Here are some different ways of asking a comparative question.

 In the examination you will have to answer one question out of three.

Questions

Higher

1   Compare the ways the poets present people in Duffy's 'Havisham', **one** poem by Armitage and **two** pre-1914 poems.

2   Answer **both** parts of the question.
    (a) Compare the ways feelings are expressed in 'Hitcher' and **one** poem by Duffy.
    (b) Compare the ways feelings are expressed in **two** pre-1914 poems.

3   Answer **both** parts of the question.
    (a) Compare the ways Clarke uses images in 'Catrin' with the way **one** of the pre-1914 poets uses images.
    (b) Compare the presentation of nature in 'Storm on the Island' and **one** other pre-1914 poem.

4   Compare the ways the writers build up tension in **two** poems from List A and **two** poems from List B:

List A	List B
Education for Leisure	My Last Duchess
Hitcher	The Laboratory
Salome	The Man He Killed
Those bastards in their mansions	Ulysses

5   Compare the ways the writers present nature in **two** poems from List A and **two** poems from List B.

List A	List B
Storm on the Island	Patrolling Barnegat
Death of a Naturalist	Sonnet: I love to see the summer
The Field Mouse	Inversnaid

Foundation

1   Compare the ways the poets present death in 'Mid-Term Break', 'On the Train', '**On My First Sonne**' and one other pre-1914 poem.

Write about:
- what the deaths are like
- how feelings are brought out
- the attitudes of the poets to the deaths
- your own response to the poems.

2   Answer **both** parts of the question.
   (a) Compare the ways Duffy and Armitage present violence in 'Salome' and 'Hitcher'.
   (b) Compare the ways in which violence is presented in 'The Man He Killed' and 'The Laboratory'.

In each part of the question write about:
- how the kinds of violence are similar and different
- the reasons for and the effects of the violence
- the language the writers use to present the violence
- your own response to the ways the poems are written.

3   Answer **both** parts of the question.
   (a) Compare the techniques which the poets use to create a speaker for 'Stealing' and 'Kid'.
   (b) Compare the ways the speaker is presented in 'The Man He Killed' and one other pre-1914 poem.

In each part of the question write about:
- what the speaker is like
- the ideas, thoughts, and feelings of the speaker
- how the language shows what the speaker is like.

4   Choose **two** poems from List A and two poems from List B and compare the ways relationships between members of different generations are presented in the poems:

List A	List B
Mid-Term Break	The Song of the Old Mother
Follower	On My First Sonne
Baby-Sitting	The Affliction of Margaret
Catrin	The Little Boy Lost or The Little Boy Found

Write about:
- ◆ what the relationships between generations are like in the poems
- ◆ the ways in which these relationships are similar and different
- ◆ the methods the poets use to show what the relationships are like
- ◆ which of the poems you like best and why.

5 Choose **two** poems from List A and **two** poems from List B. Compare the ways the writers use language interestingly to achieve their effects.

Write about:
- ◆ interesting uses of language
- ◆ the effects created by these uses of language
- ◆ how the uses of language in the poems are similar and different.

List A	List B
Havisham	On My First Sonne
Elvis's Twin Sister	The Laboratory
Kid	The Man He Killed
My father thought it	Tichborne's Elegy

How to move up the grade bands

It might help you to look at some of the grade descriptions for English Literature, because it is these that determine the mark you get. By looking at them closely you can begin to see what your targets need to be, and how you can try to reach for a grade higher than you might be getting at the moment.

Your grade, of course, relates to your answer as a whole, so it's quite difficult to give brief examples which demonstrate the achievement of a grade. However, you can see some of the skills required with the text and question in the following examples.

The question I am going to use as an example is a very broad one:

Question

How do the poets present people in 'Catrin' by Clarke, one poem by Heaney and two pre-1914 poems?

Write about:
- ◆ what the people are like
- ◆ the methods the poets use to present them
- ◆ your own response to the poems.

G grade

- ✔ simple response to text or task
- ✔ familiarity with specific part(s) of a text/reference to some detail(s)
- ✔ simple comment on meaning
- ✔ reference to language and/or method
- ✔ selection of text(s) suitable for comparison
- ✔ some features/details from one or more poems
- ✔ simple statement(s) about people
- ✔ simple comment(s) about people.

Extract from G-grade answer

Gillian Clarke writes about her daughter in Catrin. She found it hard to get on with her when she was little because she is not nice about her: 'I can remember you, child'. Seamus Heaney is sad about his dead brother in Mid-Term Break because he says: 'A four foot box, a foot for every year'.

F grade

- ✔ some response to characters/situations/ideas
- ✔ selection of appropriate material/some range of detail
- ✔ awareness of explicit meaning(s)
- ✔ simple identification of a method or an effect
- ✔ selection of material for comparison
- ✔ simple linkage in terms of ideas/meanings/techniques
- ✔ selection of appropriate material relevant to people from two or more poems
- ✔ simple comments on details of people
- ✔ some awareness of writers' methods of presenting people
- ✔ some linkage between poems, e.g. similarity or difference.

Extract from F-grade answer

Gillian Clarke writes about the difficulties of being a parent with a daughter. She writes about childbirth and when her daughter is older and wants to do things: 'May I skate in the dark for one last hour'. On the other hand Seamus Heaney writes about the death of his brother in Mid-Term Break. Ben Jonson also writes about the death of his son in On My First Sonne. Heaney makes you think about the death by mentioning the image of the 'poppy bruise'. Jonson makes you think about the death by mentioning that he is his 'first son'.

E grade

> ✔ supported response to characters/situations/ideas
> ✔ support points made/some comment on detail
> ✔ generalization(s) about meanings of texts
> ✔ some awareness of writer at work
> ✔ selection of some ideas for comparison
> ✔ selection of appropriate material relevant to people from two or more poems
> ✔ simple comment on details of people
> ✔ simple awareness of writers' methods of presenting people.

Extract from E-grade answer

Gillian Clarke shows how she is tied to her daughter. She uses the image of the 'red rope of love'. She also picks an example of the difficulties she has with her daughter when she includes her daughter's words: 'May I skate in the dark for one last hour'. Ben Jonson is also tied to his son but he doesn't give any details of his son. He writes about his sad feelings. He says he loves him and writes about his own feelings of loss: 'thou child of my right hand'. Heaney's poem is told from the brother's point of view. It tells of what he saw. He saw a small coffin and he uses the image of a 'poppy bruise'.

D grade

✔ some focus on the question
✔ explained response to characters/situations/ideas
✔ range of comments with supporting detail
✔ awareness of meaning(s), feeling(s) and attitude(s)
✔ identification of effects intended/achieved
✔ selection of material relevant for comparison
✔ structured comments on similarities/differences in terms of ideas/meanings/techniques
✔ treatment of at least three poems, including pre- and post-1914
✔ focus on presentation of people
✔ explained/sustained response to details of presentation of people
✔ identification/explanation of writers' methods of presenting people.

Extract from D-grade answer

Gillian Clarke writes about herself and her daughter in her poem. Ben Jonson writes mainly about himself though he does mention some general points about his son. Heaney shows his own reaction to the death of his brother. These are therefore all different in the way they present the people they are writing about. The poets are also different people. Clarke writes about her daughter at birth and at adolescence. She shows the tie between mother and daughter in the image of the 'red rope of love' which is the umbilical cord and also what ties them together later on. Ben Jonson writes generally about his son, calling him 'thou child of my right hand' and his 'joy' and 'lov'd boy'. Heaney is specific in Mid-Term Break because he writes about people's comments at the funeral and about what his dead brother looked like with the image of the 'poppy bruise' – poppies because of Remembrance Day.

C grade

✔ structured response to task
✔ sustained response to characters/situations/ideas
✔ effective use of details to support answer
✔ appropriate comment on meanings
✔ explanation of how effects are achieved
✔ selection of material appropriate for a range of comparison
✔ sustained focus on similarities/differences in terms of ideas/meanings/techniques
✔ treatment of at least three poems, including pre- and post-1914
✔ explained/sustained response to details of presentation of people
✔ identification/explanation of details of methods of presenting people
✔ structured/sustained comparison/contrast of presentation of people.

Extract from C-grade answer

Clarke presents the mother and the daughter in Catrin but Heaney presents a lot of people in Mid-Term Break – the speaker, his dead brother, their mother and father, old men at the funeral, other strangers, and Big Jim Evans. So whereas Clarke is looking back remembering her daughter's birth and childhood, Heaney is recreating the funeral and the mourners' reactions to his brother's death. Both are in the first person, but whereas Catrin ends with an ambiguous phrase with the daughter asking to do something which might be literal or might not (to 'skate in the dark, for one more hour'), Mid-Term Break ends with two stark images, the 'poppy bruise' and the smallness of the coffin, 'A four foot box, a foot for every year'. Catrin is about the mother's feelings about her daughter but Mid-Term Break is about many people's feelings and the reader is asked to add his or her own feelings at the end of the poem.

The Man He Killed is very different. It seems to be about one person, commenting on war by the use of direct speech, but it is actually about people in general and the kinds of bad things they do in war. Although someone is speaking in inverted commas, only parts of it are like real speech. Most of it is very formal. It is more like a moral lesson to be learned about how people can be friends in peace but enemies in war.

B grade

✔ sustained and developed response to task
✔ considered/qualified response to writers' ideas/purposes
✔ details linked to writers' intentions and purposes
✔ thoughtful consideration of meanings
✔ appreciation of writers' uses of language/structure/form
✔ thoughtful selection and consideration of material for comparison
✔ sustained and developed comparison in terms of ideas/ meanings/techniques
✔ treatment of four poems, including two pre- and two post-1914
✔ detailed and wide-ranging exploration/development of methods of presenting people
✔ sensitive/critical response to details of presentation of people
✔ developed/analytical comment on/response to details of poets' methods of presenting people
✔ evaluative comparison/contrast of details of poets' methods of presenting people.

Extract from B-grade answer

Catrin and The Man He Killed both seem to be about two people, the mother and daughter in Catrin and the soldier and his enemy in The Man He Killed, but they are both about more general experience. All mothers feel the same anxiety and struggle for separation that Clarke expresses in Catrin and Hardy wants people to consider how war makes people behave differently from the way they would behave in peacetime. Catrin is expressed through the voice of the mother, who may well be the poet ('I can remember you'), using an extended and linked metaphor of the rope to show how tied mother and daughter are. The 'red rope' may be the umbilical cord to begin with but then it is the blood link that keeps them together and also the way the daughter is still moored to her mother like a boat.

Like these two poems My Last Duchess and Follower are also told in the first person but they are very different. My Last Duchess is told in the first person and Browning gives the reader clues about the situation by having the speaker play a game with the person he is showing around. It is a mystery story where the speaker hints at the way he had his first wife murdered but disguises it. He is constantly showing off and nearly gives himself away ('I gave commands;/ Then all smiles stopped together'). He is manipulative and unpleasant. Some people think that the speaker in Follower is unpleasant too, patronizing to his ageing father, but I don't think he is. I think the simplicity of the last two lines is disguising his real feelings of sorrow about his father.

A grade

✔ analytical response to task
✔ exploratory response to writers' ideas/purposes
✔ analytical use of detail in support of argument
✔ exploration of meanings
✔ analysis of writers' use of language/structure/form and effect(s) on readers
✔ selection of a range of telling details as the basis for evaluative comparison
✔ evaluative comparison and contrast
✔ treatment of at least four poems, including two pre- and two post-1914
✔ detailed and wide-ranging exploration/development of methods of presenting people
✔ sensitive/critical response to details of presentation of people
✔ developed/analytical comment on/response to details of poets' methods of presenting people
✔ evaluative comparison/contrast of details of poets' methods of presenting people.

Extract from A-grade answer

Catrin, Follower, The Man He Killed and My Last Duchess are all first-person narratives but there are subtle differences. There is nothing to suggest that the speakers of Catrin and Follower are not the poets themselves, but the other two poems adopt different personae; there are hints of individuality in The Man He Killed with the use of a dialect words like 'nipperkin' and the suggested social status of the soldier with mention of the bars, but it is really a moral fable about the depersonalization of war.

The dramatic monologue My Last Duchess is the only one of the four which is properly a story. The Duke is trying to hoodwink his audience, but he nearly gives himself away, admitting to his murder ('I gave commands;/Then all smiles stopped together'). He is a complex and interesting character, the main focus of the poem and an unpleasant character. Some people think that the speaker in Follower is also unpleasant, resenting his father, but I do not agree. I think that it is the understated feelings about his father which are the main focus of Follower rather than his father's ageing, as he shows the inevitable differences between himself and his father, but despite these, unlike in Catrin, he cannot separate from his father.

A* grade

✔ conceptualized response to task
✔ insightful exploratory response to writer's ideas/purposes
✔ sensitive analysis of detail in support of argument
✔ convincing/imaginative interpretation of text and/or task
✔ evaluation of writers' use of language/structure/form and effect(s) on readers
✔ evaluative selection of a range of telling detail integrated into comparison
✔ evaluative comparison/contrast in terms of ideas, meanings/techniques
✔ treatment of at least four poems, including two pre- and two post-1914
✔ detailed and wide-ranging exploration/development of methods of presenting people
✔ sensitive/critical response to details of presentation of people
✔ developed/analytical comment on/response to details of poets' methods of presenting people
✔ evaluative comparison/contrast of details of poets' methods of presenting people.

Extract from A*-grade answer

The Man He Killed is a simple and strange poem. Hardy writes a poem about the depersonalization of war but does so by means of a monologue. Unlike Browning's extremely 'dramatic' dramatic monologue, Hardy's is undramatic; the language is often flat and sometimes inconsistent. The archaisms of 'Had he and I but met', the redundancy of 'some old ancient' and the inversions of 'Yes; quaint and curious war is!' appear to be universalizing techniques, but they give little sense of a real speaker and even less sense of the personality of 'my foe'. It barely presents people at all, unlike Catrin, where there is a psychological examination of the bonds between parent and child by means of a range of ambiguous metaphors. Clarke shows this bond to be powerful ('rope') but it is also painful ('red') and restricting ('tight'), even potentially life-threatening ('Tightening about my life'). Clarke shows the dangers and terrors of motherhood as well as its responsibilities. She characterizes herself fully. Heaney also characterizes himself fully; we learn a lot about him in Follower because we see what he notices about his father. While the first three stanzas appear to be describing the father, they are also presenting a view of the son who notices size, physical power (which may be metaphorical and psychological as well as actual), a hawk-like gaze (which could equally well be a glower) and a meticulous precision which could well have been threatening to the son who cannot shake his father off even when his father is old. The poem's ironic title makes us think about leaders and followers in families. Ulysses also makes the reader think about leaders and followers but in a heroic, literary and classical way. The poem is much more philosophical than the other three, even more so than Catrin, because Tennyson's interest appears to be in voyage and discovery, and in the possibility of maintaining moral integrity while opening up new horizons. It is the only one of these four poems which is about an age rather than an individual, an age seen through the eyes of an individual speaking to an unknown audience on an unknown occasion.

GLOSSARY

Alliteration	Repetition of the same consonant in words that are close together
Ambiguity	Meaning more than one thing at the same time
Antithesis	Opposition or contrast
Assonance	Repetition of the same vowel sound in words that are close together
Blank verse	Standard form of English poetry, using iambic pentameter and no rhymes
Cliché	A phrase that has become overused, so does not carry as much meaning as it once did
Conceit	Image or idea; often a comparison of things not obviously alike – e.g. the heart as a machine with cogs and wires
Colloquial	The language of everyday speech
Enjambment	Where the meaning of one line of poetry runs on to the next without punctuation at the end of the line
Extended image	The same image used several times, perhaps in slightly different ways, e.g. the rope in 'Catrin'
Extended metaphor	An extended comparison that does not use a comparison word such as 'like' or 'as'
Iambic pentameter	Ten-syllable lines divided into five groups of two syllables, the first syllable unstressed and the second stressed
Image	A picture created by words
Metaphor	A comparison made without using a comparison word such as 'like' or 'as' – saying that something is something else
Narrative	The story. A narrative poem is one that tells a story
Onomatopoeia	Where words sound like their meaning, e.g. 'buzz'
Oxymoron	Opposite statements or suggestions which are both true
Pathetic fallacy	Imagery where the weather or nature is used to describe someone's mood or feelings
Persona	A person or voice created to tell a story or poem, different from the writer
Personification	Attributing human qualities to an object or idea

Pun	A play on words, using a word with two or more meanings
Rhetorical question	A question that doesn't require an answer, used for effect
Rhyme	Two words, each at the end of a line of poetry, which sound the same or match each other. Half-rhymes are similar sounds; para-rhymes have some elements in common; sight rhymes look, but don't sound, the same
Rhyming couplet	An adjacent pair of lines with the same sound at the end
Rhythm	The beat of the line (which may vary within a line or in a poem); iambic pentameter is a commonly used rhythm
Satirize	To mock or poke fun at
Semantic field	Words related to each other by meaning (or topic)
Simile	A comparison using the words 'like' or 'as'
Sonnet	Most broadly, a poem with fourteen lines. Some poets (e.g. Shakespeare) use sonnets with a strict rhythm pattern and rhyme scheme
Stanza	A poem's division into sections, also sometimes called 'verses'
Symbolism	Where a word (or image) carries a wider meaning and stands for something much bigger
Syntactical inversion	When the grammatical parts of a sentence are in an unexpected order
Syntax	Grammar; sentence construction